Contents

favourite Writers: pages 4~29

Other favourite Writers: pages 30~31

David Almond

Born in Newcastle, David Almond grew up as part of a large family in the north-east of England. After being a student at the University of East Anglia, David took on various jobs – as a postman, labourer, hotel porter, even a brush salesman. He later became a teacher and the editor of a short-story magazine.

During the 1980s David lived for a year in a commune in Norfolk where he wrote his first stories. Now back in Newcastle and with a family of his own, David writes full time. His stories are based around places he knows, but they are full of myth and magic, which gives them their special poetic character.

In a crumbling old garage, there is an ailing magical creature, Skellig, who is being helped back to life. This award-winning book is destined to become a children's classic.

David's first novel, *Skellig*, won the 1998 Whitbread Children's Book of the Year, the Carnegie Medal and the Guardian Children's Fiction Award.

Quote

We walked over great piles of rubble, all that was left of the warehouses and workplaces. We walked over cinders and blackened earth where kids' bonfires had been. The ground was ruined, cracked, potholed. Crows hopped across the debris. A rat scuttled across our path. There was barbed wire. There were signs telling us to keep out. We scrambled across the fences and kept on walking.

From: *Heaven Eyes* (Hodder Children's Books, 2000).

SELECTED BIBLIOGRAPHY

Skellig; Kit's Wilderness; Heaven Eyes; Counting Stars; Secret Heart.

Now try reading:

The books of Janni Howker, Susan Price and Philip Ridley.

FAVOURITE Writers

by Kate Jones

an imprint of Hodder Children's Books

Titles in this series:

favourite Poets
favourite Writers

Editor: Sarah Doughty
Designer: Tessa Barwick

This edition published in 2001 by
Hodder Wayland, an imprint of
Hodder Children's Books

Reprinted in 2002

Cover permissions: (top left to bottom right): *Thief* by Malorie Blackman, illustration by David Brazell, reproduced by permission of Transworld Publishers (a division of Random House); photo supplied by Malorie Blackman; *Skellig* by David Almond published by Hodder Children's Books, cover reproduced by permission of Fletcher Sibthorp; photo supplied by David Almond; artwork by Quentin Blake, from *Mr. Magnolia*, reproduced by permission of Jonathan Cape, originally published by Red Fox (a division of Jonathan Cape); *Harry Potter and the Prisoner of Azkaban* reproduced by permission of Bloomsbury Publishing plc, 1999, cover illustration copyright Cliff Wright, 1999; photo supplied by J.K Rowling; main photo supplied by Anne Fine; *The Sheep-Pig* by Dick King-Smith, reproduced by permission of Puffin, (an imprint of Penguin Children's Books); photo supplied by Penguin Books (photography copyright Michael Dyer).

A Cataloguing record for this book is available from the British Library

ISBN 0 7502 2790 7

Printed in Hong Kong by Wing King Tong

Hodder Children's Books
A division of Hodder Headline Limited
338 Euston Road, London NW1 3BH

Your Questions . . .

Why did you become an author?

It's a kind of hunger. I wrote stories as a boy. I dreamed of seeing my books in our local library one day. I love the look of printed pages and the feel of books. The act of writing stories can be truly exciting and amazing – and it becomes more so as I go on.

Where do you get your ideas from?

From memories, from dreams, from thin air, from books I've read, from things I see, from things I hear. The images have a kind of resonance when I write them down.

What ambitions have you got now?

To continue writing new books. To keep on improving as a writer.

Which is your favourite of your own books?

A new book needs lots of care and attention. So my favourite's always the new one, currently called *Secret Heart*.

Are settings important?

The best stories, no matter how magical they might appear, take place in a real and recognizable world. I'm haunted by the north-eastern landscape that surrounds me. I love to explore it, to describe it, to set real places alongside imagined places, to expose what's beautiful and ugly, to discover what might be hiding in the shadows, to uncover seams of magic.

Advice:

Believe you can do it. Do it. Stay calm. Enjoy yourself. Writing is a form of play.

Comment:

I grew up as a writer when I turned to writing books for children. Children are demanding and perceptive readers, and I've learned so much about storytelling and the nature of the imagination. It's marvellous to have a readership whose minds are flexible, and able to consider all kinds of possibilities.

Malorie Blackman

Malorie Blackman grew up in London. She always loved reading and when she was at school wanted to be an English teacher. However, she followed a successful career in computers until she changed her career by starting to write books for children. Her first novel was published in 1990 and she has many books and awards to her name.

Some of Malorie's books reflect her Caribbean ancestry, and the detail comes from family stories not personal experience. Some demonstrate her keen grasp of technology and the ethical issues surrounding scientific advances. All of them glow with her energy, her love of life and her infectious sense of humour.

Quote

The envelope containing the three disks my uncle had given me sat conspicuously on my bedside table. I hadn't even had the chance to load them up onto Mum's PC and see what was on them yet. It was almost as if I'd been given them in another lifetime, another world – a sane, normal world where Uncle Robert was just an ordinary uncle and Mum … Mum wasn't on the run from the police …

From: *A.N.T.I.D.O.T.E.* (Corgi, 1997).

Wrongly accused of theft, an extraordinary storm suddenly whirls 12-year-old Lydia into a computer-dominated future.

SELECTED BIBLIOGRAPHY

Girl Wonder to the Rescue; Betsey Biggalow is Here!; The Marty Monster; Grandma Gertie's Haunted Handbag; Hacker; Operation Gadgetman; Thief!; A.N.T.I.D.O.T.E; Pig-Heart Boy; Lie Detectives; Animal Avengers; Not so Stupid!

Now try reading:

The books of Mary Hoffman, Jill Paton Walsh, Judith Kerr, Jacqueline Wilson.

Your Questions . . .

Why did you become an author?

Because I love, love, love to read. The thought of writing my own stories and actually seeing them in books with my name on the front was also very appealing. Plus the fact that when I was growing up, I read hundreds and hundreds of books and not one of them featured a black child like me.

Where do you get your ideas from?

By keeping my eyes and ears open and being incredibly interested (nosy!) in everyone and everything I see. Ideas come from things I read, see, conversations I have, even the way a person might act or look.

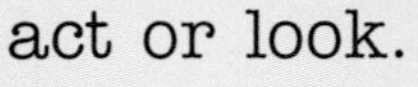

Which is your favourite of your own books?

Can I have two? *Pig Heart Boy* and *Hacker*.

What ambitions have you got now?

To be as happy as I can be.

Do you prefer writing about the Caribbean or about science?

What I love about writing is the fact that I can write whatever I like. I've only been to Barbados twice so I'm not an expert and although I love modern technology and gadgets, I certainly wouldn't like to write about them all the time.

Advice:

Read a lot. Keeping a diary is a good way of getting into the habit of writing down thoughts and feelings. Write with your own voice – don't try to copy anyone else. And don't give up.

Comment:

I write all the types of books that I love to read. Adventures, mysteries, thrillers, ghost and horror stories, family, humorous, science fiction and animal stories. In fact the only genre I haven't tried yet is Western stories! And as I'm not dead yet, who knows!

Quentin Blake

Born near London in 1932, Quentin Blake, OBE, first had drawings published when he was still at school. He has worked on over 200 books, for adults and for children, sometimes as illustrator and sometimes as the writer, too.

Quentin was head of illustration at the Royal College of Art (1978–1986), and Royal Designer for Industry (since 1981).

Quote

"It was a different life. People sent flowers to George's dressing room, and waited to see him at the stage door. Newspaper reporters interviewed Gertrude about him. Society hostesses wanted him at their parties.

"George was taken to expensive restaurants. A famous chef even invented a dish specially for him, of worms in butter sauce."

"Ugh. Fancy cooking worms."

"They weren't cooked. Frogs won't eat anything that's dead. They were alive."

From: *The Story of the Dancing Frog* (Red Fox, 1996).

SELECTED BIBLIOGRAPHY

Mister Magnolia; Quentin Blake's Nursery Rhyme Book; The Story of the Dancing Frog; Mrs Armitage on Wheels; All Join In; Cockatoos; Clown; The Quentin Blake Book of Nonsense Stories (Editor); The Green Ship; Drawing for the Artistically Undiscovered (with John Cassidy); Zagazoo; Fantastic Daisy Artichoke.

Other authors whose work Quentin Blake has illustrated:

Joan Aiken, Patrick Campbell, Roald Dahl, Sid Fleischman, Nils-Olof Franzen, Russell Hoban, Margaret Mahy, Michael Rosen, John Yeoman.

Now try reading:

The books of John Burningham, Bob Graham, Simon James, David McKee, Tony Ross.

In 1999 Quentin became the first Children's Laureate, to celebrate his massive lifetime contribution to children's literature. His quirky drawings, often with the subject suggested by minimal cartoon-like lines and sensitive water-colour washes, are distinctive and instantly recognizable.

Your Questions . . .

Why did you become an *illustrator*?

I enjoy drawing more than anything else. I like narrative, too, and designing books is also fascinating.

Where do you get your ideas from?

When I illustrate other people's books, I am using their ideas. But I also write the words for my own picture books, and I look for ideas by thinking about things I like to draw. The source of some ideas is mysterious. Where did the idea for *The Green Ship* come from, for instance?

What ambitions have you got now?

My ambition is that publishers will go on sending me stories that are even more interesting and varied than those I have illustrated so far; and that somehow or other ideas will come to me for one or two more picture books of my own.

Which is your favourite of your own books?

I think it might be *Clown*; it was both difficult and fun to do.

How did you get to draw in such a distinctive style?

My drawing is a kind of handwriting, and it is those distinctive marks that people recognize. I draw in a very economical way.

Advice:

Everyone is different, but, whether it is writing or drawing, you have to do a lot of it, and keep on doing it – that is the way to improvement.

Comment:

I did not train at art school. Later, I went to life classes and I started off just drawing as well as I could manage; one day I discovered that I could draw better if I stopped worrying about neatness and followed my instincts.

Roald Dahl

Roald Dahl's wicked sense of humour shocks some adults – but children love it! There is great variety in his books, which range from autobiography to fairy stories, but running through them is a compassion for the weak and put-upon, a hatred of the pompous, especially if they are in a position of authority, a fierce honesty and an exuberant imagination. His delight in words and language is obvious.

Quote

The air was suddenly pierced by the most frightful roar Sophie had ever heard, and she saw the Fleshlumpeater's body, all fifty-four feet of it, rise up off the ground and fall back again with a thump. Then it began to wriggle and twist and bounce about in the most violent fashion. It was quite frightening to watch.

'Eeeow!' roared the Fleshlumpeater. 'Ayeee! Oooow!'

'He's still asleep,' the BFG whispered. 'The terrible trogglehumping nightmare is beginning to hit him.'

'Serves him right,' Sophie said. She could feel no sympathy for this great brute who ate children as though they were sugar-lumps.

From: *The BFG* (Puffin, 1984/99; Everyman, 1993).

SELECTED BIBLIOGRAPHY

The Gremlins; James and the Giant Peach; Charlie and the Chocolate Factory; The Magic Finger; Fantastic Mr. Fox; Charlie and the Great Glass Elevator; Danny the Champion of the World; The Wonderful World of Henry Sugar; The Enormous Crocodile; The Twits; George's Marvellous Medicine; The BFG; Revolting Rhymes; Dirty Beasts; The Witches; Boy; The Giraffe and the Pelly and Me; Going Solo; Matilda; Esio Trot; The Vicar of Nibbleswicke; The Minpins; My Year.

Now try reading:

The books of Gillian Cross, Morris Gleitzman, C.S. Lewis, Jill Murphy, Philip Ridley, J.K. Rowling.

Born to Norwegian parents in 1916 in Llandaff, Wales, Roald Dahl lived most of his adult life in Buckinghamshire. An adventurous early life in Africa was followed by a war-time career first as a fighter pilot and then as a spy. After the war, he became a writer. He wrote many adult books and short stories as well as stories for children. He died in 1990 of leukaemia, but no book of favourite authors would be complete without him.

Quentin Blake Answers . . .

What was it like working with Roald Dahl?

I guess people may think I would say he was very difficult and demanding. Well, he was demanding, but he wasn't difficult! It is true that to begin with I did feel a bit nervous – because here was a writer who was already very famous indeed. I think he appreciated that I wanted him to be happy with the drawings; and it was not so long before we established a method of working.

How did you illustrate his books?

I would read the manuscript and make rough drawings of the incidents that I thought would make good drawings; I would also make more finished drawings of the characters. All these drawings I took down to Dahl's home in the country where he would look at them and give me his comments. Not surprisingly, he was determined that everything should be as right as possible; but this was because (unlike some authors) he wanted pictures in his books – as many as possible! – and he enjoyed looking at them.

ROALD DAHL

Boy

Tales of Childhood

Did you enjoy working with Roald Dahl?

Although in many ways Roald Dahl and I were very different characters, there was no doubt of our shared enjoyment in the humour. There was the added enjoyment for me in that every book seemed to be different. You never knew what was coming next – each time a new set of problems and opportunities. Wasn't I lucky?!

Quentin Blake.

Anne Fine

Born in 1947 in Leicester, Anne grew up with four sisters and spent her childhood poring over books in the library. As an adult, she has taught in a school and a prison, but mostly moved around with her husband and daughters – to the USA, Canada and Scotland – writing in every spare moment.

SELECTED BIBLIOGRAPHY:

The Diary of a Killer Cat; Bill's New Frock; The Country Pancake; A Sudden Puff of Glittering Smoke; How to Write Really Badly; Bad Dreams; Goggle-Eyes; Flour Babies; The Tulip Touch; Madame Doubtfire; The Book of the Banshee; Step by Wicked Step.

Now try reading:

The books of Judy Blume, Berlie Doherty, Robert Swindells, Jacqueline Wilson.

ANNE FINE Madame DOUBTFIRE

This award-winning book is also a film called Mrs. Doubtfire. *Three children of divorced parents are supervised by an adult who is closer to them than they imagine...*

Quote

'I know!' I cried. 'I know why you're so upset! I know why you're crying your eyes out! I know why you don't want to be sent home!'

She lifted two fierce, red-rimmed little eyes that burned through the gloom of the cupboard like live coals.

'Your mum's going to marry the man with grey hair!'

Her mouth fell open. I felt like Sherlock Holmes on a good day.

'And you think he's a proper creep! You've thought he was a creep all along, but, being the sweet Helly that you are, you've been too gentle and polite to say so.'

From: *Goggle-Eyes* (Puffin, 1990/93/2000).

Anne writes with sensitivity and honesty, and is not afraid to write about feelings of pain or suffering. She also has a delicious sense of humour, so her books are bubbly and great fun – as well as challenging. Anne is a winner of many awards, both here and abroad, and her work is now in twenty-eight languages. She was deservedly one of the three towering children's writers short-listed to be the first ever Children's Laureate

Your Questions . . .

Why did you become an author?

Because it's the closest you can get to reading all day. And I can write the books I would have loved simply to sit down and read – if only someone else had written them first for me!

Where do you get your ideas from?

From things I see, things I overhear, things I read. From everywhere. But the best books always seem to be ones where the hero or heroine is very like me, or someone I know well, and where either I, or someone I care about, has a particular interest in the book's subject.

Which is your favourite of your own books?

For young people, *The Angel of Nitshill Road*. I love Celeste's sheer courage and outspokenness. I like the things she does, but I would never have dared say any of them in class.

What ambitions have you got now?

The same as ever – to keep reading, to keep writing.

How can you be so funny about serious subjects?

I think that complicated matters are more interesting to write about, but I have a cheerful nature, so comedy does keep breaking through.

Advice:

Read everything. Which means making sure you're not watching more than seven hours television a week!

Comment:

I try always to think of the reader. Will they enjoy this? Will they be getting bored? I'm good at showing the world as it is, unpicking its awkwardnesses and complications. My readers often say, "Yes, that's exactly how it was for me (or someone I know)." So they find the books, not just funny, but helpful, too.

Dick King-Smith

When Dick King-Smith's book, *The Sheep-Pig*, was made into the immensely popular film, *Babe*, fans of all ages realized why children so love his books. His first book, *The Fox Busters*, came out in 1975 and already showed his trademarks – a witty way of making animals speak and behave in crazy ways, without losing their animal characteristics.

One of the writer's most famous books (right) and a still from the film Babe *(above), 1995.*

Quote

'Simple question. Why is it that we can't catch a Foxearth fowl?'

'Well, that's obvious,' replied his brother, 'they fly too well.'

'Why do they?'

'Because they've got blooming great wings, of course. Why do you ask such silly questions?'

'Sorry,' said the first speaker, 'I'm just trying like mad to think of some way in which we can outwit them.'

While the brothers had been talking, the two vixens listened. Then suddenly both sat bolt upright, ears pricked, green eyes alight, staring at each other.

From: *The Fox Busters* (Puffin, 1995/99).

SELECTED BIBLIOGRAPHY

Magnus Powermouse, Saddlebottom, Noah's Brother, The Fox Busters, Babe, A Mouse Called Wolf, Dirty Gertie Mackintosh, Sophie's Snail, Dodos are Forever, The Water Horse, Godhanger, The Crowstarver.

Now try reading:

The books of Enid Blyton, Bonnie Bryant, Jenny Dale (Puppy Patrol), Lucy Daniels (Animal Ark & Animal Ark Pets), Colin Dann, Nigel Hinton (Beaver Towers), E. B. White (Charlotte's Web).

Born in Gloucestershire in 1922, Dick served in the wartime Grenadier Guards, then farmed in Gloucestershire (until he went bankrupt), then taught for seven years. This is why he understands both animals and children so well!

Your Questions . . .

Why did you become an author?

By mistake: I had an idea for a story (*The Fox Busters*), and after about ten years of thinking about it while I was milking the cows, I wrote it and was lucky enough to have it accepted.

Where do you get your ideas from?

Out of my slightly crazy mind and memories.

Which is your favourite of your own books?

The Sheep-Pig.

What ambitions have you got now?

Not to go 'doolally', i.e. to continue to be able to think straight and go on writing.

Did you like *Babe*?

I loved it. I wasn't in the cinema for five minutes before I was grinning all over my face: the actor they'd chosen to play Farmer Hoggett was exactly the man I'd had in my mind when I wrote the story.

Advice:

READ everything you can lay your hands on. PRACTISE writing stories. SHOW them to your teacher or parent. LISTEN to their comments and their criticisms. Try not to be needlessly wordy. Everything you write should be designed to keep the pace of the story going, draw the reader on, make him or her eager to know what's going to happen next.

Comment:

I like animals, and have kept lots of them. It's such fun putting words into their mouths. I make them behave as they would in the wild or on the farm, but I allow them the gift of speech and also certain characteristics, such as courage. I also like writing silly verses.

Michael Morpurgo

Michael Morpurgo M.B.E. grew up in wartime London. At school he was thought of as rather stupid but great at rugby! He became a teacher, but the book *Poetry in the Making* by Ted Hughes made him decide to write instead. He is a great storyteller and has won international acclaim for his titles.

A violent storm brings unexpected rewards for a family in this award-winning book, inspired by the writer's annual visit to the Isles of Scilly.

Quote

"Be wild now," he whispered. "You've got to be wild. Don't come home. Don't ever come home. They'll put you behind bars. You hear what I'm saying? All my life I'll think of you." And he buried his head in the lion's neck and heard the greeting groan from deep inside him. He stood up. "I'm going now," he said. "Don't follow me. Please don't follow me." And Bertie clambered down off the kopje and walked away.

From: *The Butterfly Lion* (HarperCollins, 1996; Viking, 1997).

SELECTED BIBLIOGRAPHY

Cockadoodle-doo; Mr Sultana!; Wombat Goes Walkabout; The Butterfly Lion; Escape from Shangri-La; Albertine; Goose Queen; Martians at Mudpuddle Farm; Mum's the Word; The War of Jenkins' Ear; The Ghost of Grania O'Malley; King of the Cloud Forests; Farm Boy; Kensuke's Kingdom.

Now try reading:

The books of Joan Aiken, Nina Bawden, Michael Foreman, Leon Garfield, Alan Garner (for older children), Ursula le Guin, Ann Holm (I Am David), Michelle Magorian, Philippa Pearce, Ian Serraillier.

Michael lives in Devon and, with his wife Clare, he runs the charity, Farms for City Children. Michael's books have gripping story-lines and many are based on the Devon farm he loves so well. Many are set in historical time periods.

Your Questions . . .

Why did you become an author?

When I was teaching I found that I loved telling my stories to the children in my class. So one day I decided to write a story down.

Where do you get your ideas from?

From the world around me, from what I see and hear every day. I suppose what I do is to weave actual events together by dreaming them into one.

Which is your favourite of your own books?

Kensuke's Kingdom.

What ambitions have you got now?

I'd like to have just two or three of my books to become a part of the lives of children growing up – for a long, long time.

Does Farms for City Children help you as an author?

Immensely. Working alongside children I watch them and listen to them. They are my inspiration. I also try my stories out on them when I read to them in the evenings. I soon know if they like them or not.

Advice:

Read a lot and widely, live a rich and varied life, never stop looking and listening and learning. Don't be in a hurry to write. And when you do, write with your heart as well as your head.

Comment:

Writing is only a part of my life: an important part; but I would not want it to encroach on the living of my life. The living comes before the writing.

Terry Pratchett

Terry Pratchett grew up in Buckinghamshire. By the age of 13 he had sold his first story and bought a typewriter with the proceeds. He left school at 17 and went to work as a journalist. He had his first book published in 1974 and since then has had 18 million copies of his books sold worldwide.

His books appeal to all ages, though some are more obviously for younger children. Terry has a great sense of humour. If you enjoy language and playing with words, you'd like Terry's *Discworld* series, which is highly imaginative.

Quote

Johnny hesitated. I could turn around now, he thought, and go home. And if I turn around, I'll never find out what happens next. I'll go away and I'll never know why it happened now and what would have happened next. I'll go away and grow up and get a job and get married and have children and become a grandad and retire and take up bowls and go into Sunshine Acres and watch daytime television until I die, and I'll never know.

From: *Johnny and the Dead* (Doubleday, 1993, Corgi 1994).

SELECTED BIBLIOGRAPHY

Diggers, Truckers; The Carpet People; Only You Can Save Mankind; Johnny and the Dead; Johnny and the Bomb; The Colour of Magic; The Light Fantastic; Mort; Wyrd Sisters; Pyramids; Guards! Guards!

Now try reading:

The books of J. R. R. Tolkien, Mary Norton (The Borrowers), Robert Rankin, Sylvia Waugh (The Mennyms), Douglas Adams, Tom Holt, Peter Dickinson, Philippa Pearce.

The Discworld *novels are regular bestsellers. In this book, Mort takes an unlikely job as Death's apprentice; with fascinating consequences.*

Your Questions . . .

Why did you become an author?

It just seemed to happen naturally. I got filled up by a lot of books and then I overflowed.

Where do you get your ideas from?

Who knows? But I read a lot and pay attention to the world. Most ideas I make up, by sitting and thinking hard. They don't always drop out of the sky!

Which is your favourite of your own books?

Oh dear. *Mort*, I suppose.

What ambitions have you got now?

I've never really had ambitions, but I would like to visit Mars one day.

Have you always looked at ordinary things in a wacky way?

I prefer to think that I look at ordinary things in a very clear and logical way, but it's not the logic that people normally use. A lot of things we call 'ordinary' are really rather strange.

Advice:

The important thing to remember is that, unless you are a genius, writing isn't easy. You have to train yourself. You have to realize that grammar, punctuation and spelling aren't things that just happen to other people. You have to read other writers and work out how they achieve their effects. You need an inquisitive mind and wide reading and viewing habits.

Comment:

Inspiration doesn't find you, you find it. Mainly by sitting down and writing about anything that crosses your mind until some kind of magic starts to happen. It worked for me!

Philip Pullman

Philip Pullman travelled widely as a young child, although his later childhood was spent in Wales. After university he taught first in middle schools, then he taught teachers in Oxford, where he now lives; specializing in the Victorian novel, traditional tales and how stories and pictures fit together.

Philip is a brilliant story-teller. Sometimes you are swept away in a high-spirited, exuberant, action-packed tale; sometimes the richness and breadth of imagination and mystery make the reading compulsive. Either way, it's real torch-under-the-bedclothes stuff!

Quote

A rending, splintering sound made them all look back at the house. A window at ground level, obviously opening on a cellar, was being wrenched apart with a crash of glass and a screech of tearing wood. The sentry who'd followed Iorek Byrnison into the house came running out and stood to face the cellar window, rifle at his shoulder; and then the window tore open completely, and out there climbed Iorek Byrnison, the bear in armour. Without it he was formidable. With it, he was terrifying.

From: *Northern Lights* (Scholastic, 1995/98).

SELECTED BIBLIOGRAPHY:

The Gas Fitter's Ball; I was a Rat!; Count Karlstein; The Broken Bridge; The Butterfly Tattoo; The Ruby in the Smoke; The Shadow in the North; The Tiger in the Well; The Firework-Maker's Daughter; Clockwork, Northern Lights (Dark Materials 1); The Subtle Knife (Dark Materials 2).

Now try reading:

The books of J. R. R. Tolkien, Mary Norton (The Borrowers), Robert Rankin, Sylvia Waugh (The Mennyms), Douglas Adams, Tom Holt, Peter Dickinson, Philippa Pearce.

Only one person knows the truth when Roger insists he was once a rat, rampaging through the sewers. An action-packed adventure from this popular writer.

Your Questions . . .

Why did you become an author?

I became "an author" because I started to write. But if you'd asked me "Why do you write?", however, I might not be able to tell you.

Where do you get ideas from?

I subscribe to IDEAS R US™. For £25 a month I get thirty ideas, new and unused, success guaranteed. You can get second-hand more cheaply, but they don't come with a guarantee, and they wear out. Alternatively, you can just go about with your eyes and ears open. And read. And think.

Which is your favourite of your own books?

I haven't written it yet. I shan't know until I've written all the books I'm going to write, which I hope will take me a very long time.

How do you make your stories so exciting?

They just happen like that – I don't plan them in advance.

Advice:

My advice is to use your head. You have a brain which is the most complicated thing in the known universe. It is capable of storing an infinity of memories, inventing things that have never been known before, and giving enormous and lasting delight and benefit to yourself and others. Use as much of it as you can reach. Find out what you're here to do, and do it until you are worn out or you have completed the task.

J. K. Rowling

Joanne Rowling (J.K!) grew up in Chepstow, Gwent and wrote her first book when she was six. She studied French and Classics at Exeter university, then worked for Amnesty International in London.

The Harry Potter idea started as an idea on a train journey and then was written in cafés and pubs in London, north Portugal (where she taught English as a foreign language) and Edinburgh, where she now lives with her daughter. They have taken the world by storm, appealing to both adults and children with their mixture of good old-fashioned school-story fun, adventure, humour and magic invention.

In this book, Harry is in his third year of Hogwarts School of Witchcraft and Wizardry, and the sinister guards of Azkaban have been called in to guard the school...

Quote

The pages of the diary began to blow as though caught in a high wind, stopping halfway through the month of June. Mouth hanging open, Harry saw that the little square for June the thirteenth seemed to have turned into a miniscule television screen. His hands trembling slightly, he raised the book to press his eye against the little window, and before he knew what was happening, he was tilting forwards; the window was widening, he felt his body leave his bed and he was pitched headfirst through the opening on the page, into a whirl of colour and shadow.

From: *Harry Potter and the Chamber of Secrets* (Bloomsbury, 1998/99).

AUTHOR BIBLIOGRAPHY

Harry Potter and the Philosopher's Stone; Harry Potter and the Chamber of Secrets; Harry Potter and the Prisoner of Azkaban.

Now try reading:

Jill Murphy, Philip Pullman, Ursula le Guin.

Your Questions . . .

Why did you become an author?

I have never wanted to be anything but a writer. It has been my ambition since I was about six years old and completed my first 'book' – a story about a rabbit called *Rabbit* (with illustrations by the author).

Where do you get your ideas from?

This is the hardest question to answer. They come from somewhere inside my head, that's as precise as I can be.

Which is your favourite of your own books?

Harry Potter and the Prisoner of Azkaban, partly because I liked the plot, and partly because it's the first time Professor Lupin appears and he's one of my favourite characters.

What ambitions have you got now?

The usual and impossible one, to write a book with which I am entirely satisfied, of which I wouldn't want to change a single word. It's never happened yet, and I doubt it ever will.

What is the most magical thing that has ever happened to you?

There are two contenders for this: firstly, the way Harry Potter strolled into my mind on a delayed train journey when I was thinking about nothing except how much I wanted to get home; secondly, the birth of my daughter, when after eleven hours' labour I looked up and saw a real baby – who knows why it seemed such a miracle to me, but it did.

Jeremy Strong

Jeremy Strong grew up in south-east London and from the age of eight wanted to be a writer. After university he started to write but didn't earn very much money so decided to be a primary school teacher. Whilst teaching he got his first stories published. Today Jeremy writes full-time.

The secret of his success can be summed up as follows: Take some ordinary modern children and then ask them "What if..?" questions, with an impish gleam in the eye; and you will understand the appeal of Jeremy Strong's imaginative, entertaining and funny stories.

Quote

"Do you want to try again?" the voice was quiet and firm.

"Who are you?" Danny demanded.

"Starstriker? My bike?" Danny looked at his BMX. No that wasn't possible. "You can't be," said Danny, beginning to feel rather stupid talking to thin air.

"Oh. Why not?"

Danny shrugged. "Bikes don't talk!" He wrinkled his nose.

"Oh. I'll shut-up then. Goodbye."

There was a silence, while Danny thought.

From: *Starbiker* (A & C Black, 1986).

SELECTED BIBLIOGRAPHY

I'm Telling You, They're Aliens; Problems with a Python; Pirate Pandemonium; The Karate Princess; There's a Viking in my Bed; Lightning Lucy; Fatbag the Demon Vacuum Cleaner; My Dad's Got an Alligator!; The Indoor Pirates; The Hundred-Mile-an-Hour Dog; The Desperate Adventures of Sir Rupert and Rosie Gusset; Dinosaur Pox.

Now try reading:

The books of Allan Ahlberg, Terry Deary, Nick Warburton, Jacqueline Wilson.

On the day of the fancy dress party the school is invaded by aliens from the planet Gobble. This is one of Hodder Wayland's storybooks from a prizewinning writer.

Your Questions . . .

Why did you become an author?

You can make anything happen when you write a story. It's magic! I have always enjoyed making things happen in my head and writing about them. I was lucky when I was eight to have a teacher who made me feel that writing was something I could do well. I wasn't much good at anything else.

Where do you get your ideas from?

Everywhere; from things I see, odd words, dreams, my own experiences, history, even from nowhere at all.

What ambitions have you got now?

When I write a new story I try to make it better than anything I have done before. I am still learning how to write stories. I hope one day I will write something that will still be making people laugh a hundred years from now.

Which is your favourite of your own books?

The Hundred Mile an Hour Dog.

Have you always had a zany sense of humour?

Yes. I grew up in a family that loved word play and using words to make others laugh.

Advice:

Don't give up trying. The moment you give up you have no chance of success.

Comment:

I write the kind of stories I wanted to read when I was nine or ten: stories that would give me a bit of excitement, lots of laughs and make me feel happy.

Robert Swindells

Robert Swindells left school at 15 and went to work at a local newspaper. Two years later he joined the RAF as an airman and spent several years working abroad. Since leaving he has had jobs as a shopworker, an engineer and a bookbinder before becoming a teacher.

Robert is now a full-time writer and lives on the Yorkshire Moors. He writes with vigour and idealism about present day issues which affect us all, but his books are not moralizing or heavy because he is a born story-teller with a gift for characterization.

SELECTED BIBLIOGRAPHY

The Go-Ahead Gang; Voyage to Valhalla; Room 13; Dracula's Castle; Nightmare Stairs; World-Eater; Peril in the Mist; Stone Cold; Daz 4 Zoe; Brother in the Land; Smash!; Abomination; Dosh.

Now try reading:

The books of Anne Fine, Margaret Mahy, Jacqueline Wilson.

Quote

Oh yes, I know it's far-fetched. I realise that it was months before I could get my head round it but, you see, the evidence was all there. I knew the layout of the cottage at Nine Beeches, though I'd never been inside. I knew its loft used to be known as the Glory Hole. I knew Grandad Rodwell's first name – Bob – though nobody had ever used the name in my hearing. And I knew exactly what had happened to Grandma Elizabeth the night they bombed Viner's – I'd seen it, felt it, without ever leaving my seat in Mr. Newell's class at Cutler's Hill Primary.

From: *Nightmare Stairs* (Yearling, 1998).

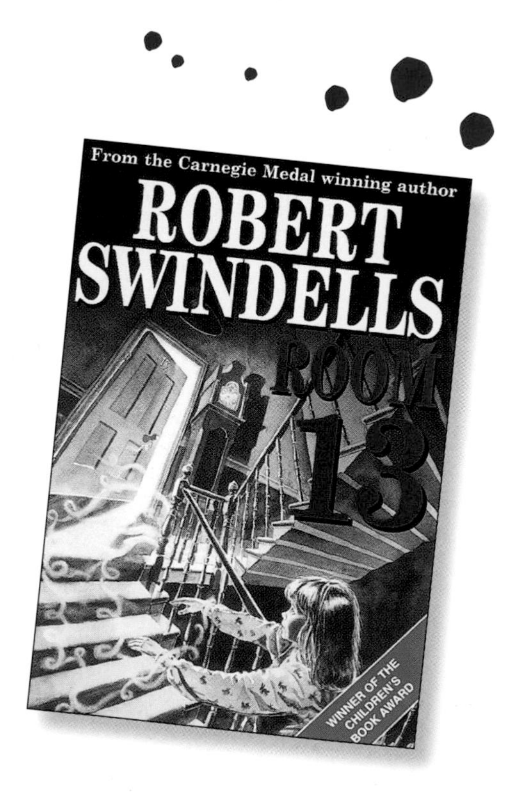

Winner of the 1990 Children's Book Award; this is a spine-tingling tale about a house in Whitby – a house with a secret; based around a room that may not exist, called Room 13.

Your Questions . . .

Why did you become an author?

I fell in love with books when I was eight and wanted to have a go myself.

Where do you get your ideas from?

Ideas are all around, but not everyone sees them. Maybe writers of fiction have a sort of antenna that picks up ideas, projects them on a screen inside the skull. It feels like that.

Which is your favourite of your own books?

Room 13.

What ambitions have you got now?

All of my personal ambitions have been fulfilled. I have an ambition for the world, which is that we all might learn to live together in peace, sharing what our planet provides.

How do you do the research for your books?

By reading. I might travel to a place I'm going to set a story in, to see what it's like, take snapshots. For *Stone Cold* I slept out for three nights in London.

Advice:

Read, read, read. You'll notice how authors have different ways of writing: their own style. Choose a style you enjoy and have a go at writing something in that style. It's not copying, it's experimenting. Write your own story on the subject you're most interested in. Gradually you'll develop your own voice as it is called. Listen to constructive advice but ignore people who try to put you down.

Comment:

I write in the hope of hooking young people on reading, because reading changes lives.

Jacqueline Wilson

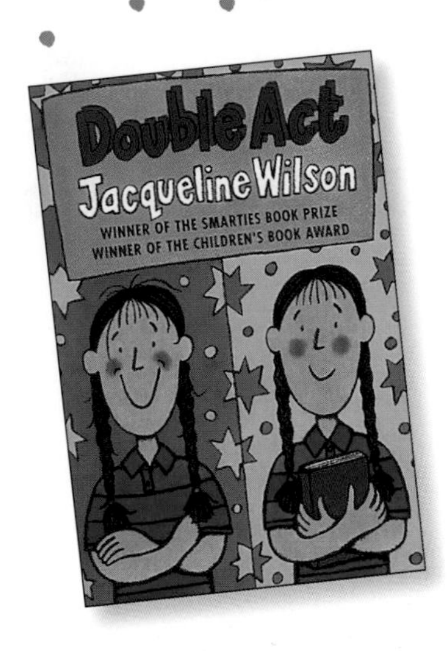

A hilarious story from this award-winning writer – about twins, Ruby and Garnet, and how they cope after their mother's death.

Jacqueline Wilson has been a writer ever since she was 17, when she went to work on the teenage magazine, *Jackie*. She has written books for adults but for the last twenty years most of her writing has been for young people and has won her many awards. She runs workshops for children in creative writing. She lives in Surrey and has one grown-up daughter.

SELECTED BIBLIOGRAPHY

The Dinosaur's Packed Lunch; The Mum-Minder; My Brother Bernadette; Monster Eyeballs; The Story of Tracy Beaker; The Suitcase Kid; The Bed and Breakfast Star; Double Act; Bad Girls; The Lottie Project; The Illustrated Mum; Glubbslyme.

Now try reading:

The books of Judy Blume, Anne Fine, Pete Johnson, Jeremy Strong, Robert Swindells, Sue Townsend, Jean Ure.

Quote

Marigold had put the light on. It was so bright I could see nothing at first. I clung to her, my eyes little cracks in my face. I could smell the drink on her breath but she still seemed fine, though she was trembling. I held her tight but she wasn't concentrating on me.

'Star! Star, sit up, my sweet. There!' Marigold leant across me and brushed Star's hair out of her eyes. 'Star, I'd like you to meet someone.' Marigold's voice was so shaky with excitement she could hardly get the words out. 'It's Micky, Star, your father!'

From: *The Illustrated Mum* (Doubleday, 1999; Yearling 2000).

Jacqueline has a sensitive understanding of modern children, the way they live and the problems they face. Her books are very much centred around the various situations children find themselves in. In addition she has a delightful sense of fantasy and a good sense of humour. Jacqueline has also written a series of crime novels and several plays for radio.

Your Questions . . .

Why did you become an author?

Because I always loved making up stories and playing pretend games when I was young.

Where do you get your ideas from?

I don't know! They just seem to pop into my head.

Which is your favourite of your own books?

Double Act. It is about identical twin sisters, Ruby and Garnet.

What ambitions do you have now?

I'd like to write lots more books – and I'd love to become the star of my local line dancing team!

Do boys enjoy your books as well as girls?

Lots of boys tell me they enjoy my books, even the ones that have lots of girly things in them. I think it's maybe because they're quite funny books about modern subjects. Boys don't want to miss out!

Advice:

I think it's a great idea to keep a diary. When it comes to writing stories I'd just relax and tell it as it comes – don't try too hard!

Comment:

I love writing books for children. It means so much to me that hundreds of children write me letters each week telling me all about themselves and the books they've enjoyed reading.

Other favourite Writers

There are literally hundreds of wonderful authors for you to read and enjoy. Here are some who are no longer alive, but whose books remain firm favourites.

Enid Blyton

Born in 1897 in London, Enid Blyton grew up in Beckenham. Enid was a musical child and wanted to be a pianist, but she loved reading, too. When she grew up she studied to be a kindergarten teacher, but soon writing took over. She wrote over 600 books and died in 1968. Adult critics find her books sexist and outdated, but they have always remained popular with children. Her books include the Famous Five series, the Secret Seven series, the Mystery series, Adventure series, school stories e.g. *Malory Towers*, *St. Clare's* and *Noddy*, for younger readers.

Henrietta Branford

Henrietta Branford was born in India in 1946. Her love of the countryside formed a key source of ideas for her books. She didn't start writing until she was about 40 years old. She had started to write part-time for a local newspaper and this gave her the confidence to write books for children and some of her books started to win prizes. In her 9-year career as an author she wrote over 20 books for all ages. She died of cancer in 1999. An award has been set up in her memory to celebrate an outstanding first novel for young people. Her books include: *Fire, Bed and Bone*, *The Fated Sky*, *Dimanche Diller*, *White Wolf*, *Spacebaby* and *Ruby Red*.

Kenneth Grahame

Kenneth Grahame was born in Edinburgh in 1859. His lasting appeal is based on just one book, *The Wind in the Willows,* rediscovered by each generation of children. The characters are people we all know, but they are animals, too. Humour, adventure, friendship and a magical depiction of the countryside, developed from stories which Grahame told to his son. Later in his life, Grahame and his wife moved back to the area around Pangbourne which had inspired *The Wind in the Willows*. He died there in 1932.

C. S. Lewis

C.S. Lewis was born in 1898 outside Belfast. He gained a Triple First at Oxford and followed a distinguished academic career becoming a tutor at Magdalen College from 1925–54, where he was a contemporary of Tolkien. In 1954 he became professor of Medieval & Renaissance Literature at Cambridge. In 1956 he married Joy Gresham, an American poet who admired his work, but died four years later. He lived until 1963. For children, his enormously popular books are the Narnia series, starting with *The Lion, The Witch and The Wardrobe*.

J. R. R. Tolkien

J.R.R Tolkien was born in 1892 at Bloemfontain in South Africa but later settled in England, near Birmingham. He went to King Edward's School in Birmingham where he gained distinctions in classics. He was fascinated by language and invented special languages for 'fairy' or 'elvish' people to use. He loved the rural landscape of his childhood, too. He gained a First in English at Oxford. After the war he worked on the New English Dictionary and began to write *Silmarillon*, while working at Leeds and Oxford universities. For his four children he wrote *The Father Christmas Letters*, then *The Hobbit* and *Lord of the Rings* which took 12 years to complete. He died in 1973.

Go to any library or book shop and you will have a feast of reading to enjoy by authors writing today. Here are five to look out for but there are many, many more!

Peter Dickinson

Peter Dickinson was chosen as one of the three authors short-listed for the first ever Children's Laureate because of the range and brilliance of his books for children. He spent the first seven years of his life in Africa before returning to, and growing up in England. He was called up into the army shortly after the Second World War, then went to Cambridge. He then worked on a magazine and started writing books at the age of 40. His first wife died after their family grew up, but he married again. This breadth of his experience and emotion is reflected in the warmth and depth of his thought-provoking books: *The Kin, A Bone from a Dry Sea, Eva, Time and the Clock Mice.*

Brian Jacques

Brian Jacques is a Liverpudlian. His early years were during the Second World War, when Liverpool was heavily bombed. He read to escape from the harsh reality around him and when he left school, at 15, he went to sea as a sailor in the hope of visiting all the exciting places he had read about. But he didn't see much from the dock so he travelled through a variety of other jobs! Brian is musical and as well as enjoying opera he sings folk music. He started writing humorous monologues and this led to a radio show and so to writing books, which he loves and which gives him freedom to explore ideas. His characters, like their writer, enjoy adventures and a good laugh! He has written the Redwall books which include *Redwall, Mossflower* and *Mattimeo*.

Jan Mark

Jan Mark grew up and went to school in Ashford, Kent, before studying art in Canterbury. She worked for several years as an art teacher and visits schools regularly even now that she is a full-time writer. She spent two years as writer-in-residence at Oxford Polytechnic and still lives in Oxford. She writes excellent short stories as well as novels. Her quick ear and sharp eye show in fast funny dialogue and an acute observation of people's behaviour (particularly when they are behaving badly!). Her books are entertaining, warm, witty and thoughtful. She has written *Nothing to be Afraid Of*, *Thunder and Lightnings, The Twig Thing* and *The Sighting*.

Philippa Pearce

Philippa Pearce's father was a miller in Cambridgeshire, so she grew up in the country. She graduated from Cambridge during the War and started work as a civil servant, but also wrote scripts for BBC school radio and worked as an editor for a publisher. Gradually she wrote more and more of her own books. Her husband died soon after their daughter was born; and Philippa and her little girl moved back to Cambridgeshire, where she still lives today. Her books have a timeless quality and carry an utter conviction in the power of the imagination. She has written: *Tom's Midnight Garden, The Battle of Bubble and Squeak, A Dog So Small, The Way to Sattin Shore.*

R. L. Stine

R.L. Stine is an author whom children love but not all adults share their taste for horror! He grew up in Ohio, USA, and started writing and drawing comics and joke books when he was seven. After university he moved to New York City, working on magazines, especially a humorous magazine for children called 'Bananas'. He wrote jokey books, too, but it was in 1986 when he wrote his first really scary book, *Blind Date*, that he realized he had found the theme many children just love. His books have sold millions of copies worldwide, in 16 languages. He has written: the Goosebumps series, e.g. *Brain Juice* and the Fear Street series, e.g. *Silent Night*.

Acknowledgements

The Publishers would like to thank the following publishers and illustrators who allowed us to use their material in this book:

Bloomsbury Publishing plc for the jacket cover of *Harry Potter and the Prisoner of Azkaban*, published by Bloomsbury Publishing plc, in 1999, illustration copyright Cliff Wright, 1999; Egmont Children's Books for *The Wreck of Zanzibar*, written by Michael Morpurgo, illustrations copyright Christian Birmingham, 1995, published by Heinemann Young Books and Mammoth, imprints of Egmont Children's Books Ltd, London and used with permission; David Mostyn for *Aliens in School* (Hodder Wayland); Puffin (Penguin Books Ltd) for *Boy*, *Madame Doubtfire* and *The Sheep-Pig*; Jonathan Cape (published by Red Fox) for the illustration from *Mr. Magnolia* by Quentin Blake and for the jacket cover *Clown,* also illustrated by Quentin Blake; Fletcher Sibthorp for *Skellig* (Hodder Children's Books); Transworld (a division of the Random House Group Ltd) for *Double Act* (Nick Sharratt); *I Was a Rat* (Peter Bailey), *Mort*, *Thief* (Derek Brazell) and *Room 13* (Mark Robertson).

For photographs: David Almond 5; Malorie Blackman 7; Anne Fine 13; Egmont Children's Books 17; Penguin Books Ltd 11, 15 (copyright Michael Dyer Associates); Philip Pullman 21; J.K. Rowling 23; Jeremy Strong 26; Robert Swindells (copyright Paul Wilkinson Photography) 27; Topham Picturepoint 9, 19; Transworld 29; Universal (courtesy Kobal Collection) 14.

If you are interested in book reviews and information about authors look for them in these three specialist magazines:

'Young Writer' magazine, the magazine written by and for young writers. Write to Glebe House, Weobley, Herefordshire, HR4 8SD. Tel. 01544 318 901

http://www.mystworld.com/youngwriter

There are three issues a year and each has an interview with a top author as well as much other information about books to read, alongside the writing and writing advice.

'Books for Keeps' – an excellent magazine of reviews of children's books. Write to: 6 Brightfield Road, Lee, London. SE12 8QF. Tel. 020 8852 4953

'Carousel' – the magazine of The Federation of Children's Book Groups; includes book reviews. Write to: 7 Carrs Lane, Birmingham B4 7TG. Tel. 0121 643 6411

Other information about authors can be found direct from their publishers. Write a polite letter to their Children's Marketing department. If you write to an author c/o their publisher your letter will be forwarded and, who knows, you might even get a reply! Addresses for publishers can be found in sources such as the *Writers and Artists' Yearbook* and *The Writer's Handbook*.

The BEST way to find out about an author, however, is to read all their books! Make up your own mind.